THE BONA BOOK OF JULIAN AND SANDY

Julian and Sandy were first unleashed upon an unsuspecting public in April 1964 in a new radio show called *Round the Horne.* They reflected the new permissiveness of the time, and their irrepressibly irreverent high spirits made them instant favourites. The show itself was immensely popular, attracting an audience of around 9 million listeners per week, and in 1967 it won the Writers' Guild of Great Britain Award for the best comedy script. Since then Julian and Sandy have become as much a part of the pantheon of radio's great comic characters as Colonel Chinstrap, Eccles and Bluebottle, and extracts from the show are still frequently broadcast.

The BONA BOOK of
Julian & Sandy

The BONA BOOK of

Julian & Sandy

Adapted from the Award-Winning Radio Show, Round the Horne

by
BARRY TOOK AND MARTY FELDMAN

Illustrations by
Arthur Horner

Robson Books

FIRST PUBLISHED IN GREAT BRITAIN IN 1976 BY ROBSON BOOKS LTD., 28 POLAND STREET, LONDON W1V 3DB.
ISBN 0 903895 70 6

Computer typeset by Input Typesetting Ltd, London SE1.
Printed in Great Britain by Hazell Watson & Viney Ltd, Aylesbury, Bucks

For
DAVID ATTENBOROUGH
who ought to know better

Foreword

When we invented Julian and Sandy for *Round the Horne* in 1964, we'd no idea how popular they would become, or how their fey but knowing camp chat would spread from a limited circle of aficionados in show business to become a national institution, not to say menace.

In the hands of Kenneth Williams (Sandy) and Hugh Paddick (Julian) they grew quickly like a pair of busy lizzies into major comic creations, and no characters in *Round the Horne* could follow them. After a few abortive attempts to put them in new roles – at one time we had them working for MI5 in the 'Kenneth Horne, Master Spy' spoofs, and a quickly thwarted attempt to write them out altogether, we bowed fairly gracefully to the inevitable, and Julian and Sandy remained top of the *Round the Horne* bill to the end of its run.

Why were they successful? Well, a lot of the credit must go to Hugh and Kenneth for the skill with which they handled the dialogue, and to Kenneth Horne, whose very ordinariness when chatting to them made the characters somehow safe. They were always optimistic – rather like a pair of precious Mr. Micawbers waiting for something bizarre to turn up – and such innuendo as there was in the dialogue seemed acceptable with the benign Horne, representing the rest of us, there to referee.

We wrote Julian and Sandy with care and, indeed, love, because wayward and outrageous as they often were, you couldn't help loving them. Well, *we* did, and we hope you will enjoy this re-creation of some of their many adventures.

BARRY TOOK and MARTY FELDMAN

JULIAN Hullo – I'm Julian and this is my friend, Sandy.

SANDY How bona to vada your dolly old eek. . . . 'Ere – who're you talking to?

JULIAN The reader.

SANDY What reader?

JULIAN The omi or palone who's having a vada at this book.

SANDY Oh, I see. I thought you'd gone strange for a minute. No – of course. Well, reader, here it is, out in the open at last.

JULIAN Um. Nice.

SANDY The Memoirs of Julian and Sandy. The full story – now it can be told! We shall blurt it all out. We shall be fearless and probing . . . we shall rip the lid off.

JULIAN Here, wait a minute, you're not going to tell them about Tangiers?

SANDY Oh yes, of course – I'd forgotten. You had a nasty experience in Tangiers, didn't you?

JULIAN I'd rather not mention it. The memory still hurts. Besides, I'm shy.

SANDY It's your shyness that's always held you back. Go on – get it off your chest. Purge yourself. You'll feel better. Besides, it's smut that sells. That's what the publisher said when he approached us. He said: 'What Robson Books are always looking for is something fresh, vital, socially significant, pungent, limpid and smutty.'

JULIAN Is that what he said, that Mr. Robson?

SANDY Yes, we've all got his number, ducky. Just look at his Spring List . . . it's a disgrace.

JULIAN Forthcoming *Navels?*

SANDY That's a misprint. Probably had them done on the cheap.

JULIAN I'll say he did. Look – *Lady Chitterling's Liver, Withering Hoots* – and look what they've done to *The Carpetbaggers!*

SANDY And have a vada at this blurb – 'Her colour was wrong but men desired her. Proud, haughty, untamed – many possessed her but none could break her restless spirit. . . . *Who was the man with the whip?*'

JULIAN Sounds kinky. What's the book?

SANDY Anna Sewell's *Black Beauty.*

JULIAN Here, it reminds me of when we was between acting jobs – filling in – in that place near the British Museum, Bona Books. Do you remember when that Kenneth Horne came in and showed us his manuscript?

SANDY Remember? It's as if it was yesterday. . . .

The scene changes and we are in the editorial offices of Bona Books, a small but nonetheless seedy publishing house near the British Museum.

Bona Books

SANDY Hello, Mr. Horne. What brings you trolling in here?

HORNE I've written a book and I thought you might be interested in it.

JULIAN What's it called?

HORNE *The Life Cycle Of The Water Vole.*

SANDY It don't strike me as being particularly racy, offhand. Still, maybe we can do something with it. Let's have a vada. Hmm – it's a bit dull, isn't it?

HORNE Well, not much happens to a water vole.

SANDY Well, you have to *make* it happen. Look at your description of the hero – I quote: 'A small grey furry creature'. How is your reader going to identify with that? You want to make him big and butch, with bulging biceps, his shirt slashed open to his waist, and an unruly lock of tousled hair falling over his bronzed forehead.

JULIAN And you don't call him 'the water vole' – you have to personalize. Give him a name – like Rock or Tab or Dorian.

SANDY And you have to dramatize it – 'Who was this water vole? Nobody knew where he came from, but nothing was ever the same after he'd been there – women desired him –'

HORNE What? A water vole?

JULIAN You have to have a bit of sex in it – something like – this is just off the top of me head – 'Dorian's hot muzzle pressed against her furry cheek. "You're my kind of water vole," he murmured.'

SANDY 'They tumbled back, panting, onto the river bed. Her firm young haunches strained against the madras cotton of her blouse. "Have there been others?" Dorian murmured. "There was a field mouse once," she replied, "but it was never like this." ' You got the idea, then? What we want is four hundred pages of passionate water voles slaking their animal desires. 'Course, you'll have to change the title.

JULIAN Yes. We'll call it – *Vole Flanders, The Story of an Eighteenth-Century Water Slut.*

SANDY Fantabulosa!!

JULIAN It got printed in the end, but of course it never got into the best-seller list. As a matter of fact, it was remaindered on the day of publication but by then Sandy and me had moved on. We'd gone into the film business. We had a little lattie up an alley off Wardour Street. We called ourselves Bona Prods., and you wouldn't credit it but before we had time to turn round, that Mr. Horne had turned up again. Actually, we were pleased to see him as things had been a bit slack after our film *Motor Cycle Au Pair Boy* got panned by the critics. It starred our friend Gordon, and I thought he took his part lovely but you know how the film business is. If you haven't got Michael Caine in it you're done for. So, when Mr. Horne appeared on our half-landing that day, Sandy and me was more than happy to show him round and tell him of our hopes and desires – well, some of them. Sandy went straight to the point.

Bona Prods

SANDY	Mr. Horne – we are in the forefront of your Nouvelle Vague. That's your actual French.
JULIAN	It means we are of the New Wave.
HORNE	And very nice it looks on you, too.
JULIAN	Yes.
SANDY	You see, we've got a small independent unit.
JULIAN	We are the Cecil B's of the sixteen de mille. Small budget pictures, really.
HORNE	Would I have vada'd any of them, do you think?
SANDY	Oh – he's got all the palare, hasn't he?
JULIAN	I wonder where he picks it up.
SANDY	You may have vada'd one of our tiny bijou masterpiecettes, heartface. We made *Funny Eek, My*

Fair Palone. And then we done one on Chopin and his love for George Sanders.

HORNE Shouldn't that be George Sand?

SANDY He's right, you know. He's not wrong – he's right. I told Jule that, but he wouldn't listen.

JULIAN No wonder Rock Hudson turned the part down.

HORNE I take it you're engaged in something pretty exciting at the moment.

JULIAN No, not really. We're just standing here with our hands on our hips, talking to you. . . .

HORNE Oh – bold! Very bold.

SANDY I wonder where he spends his evenings? Oh, you mean *subjects* – well, frankly, Mr. Horne, at the moment we are dickering, aren't we, Jule?

JULIAN Yes. We're dickering. We've got one or two germs and we're dickering with them. We was thinking of a Biblical subject – in fact I was up all last night working on me outline.

SANDY Show it to Mr. Horne – show him your outline.

JULIAN Well, how I see it is this –

SANDY This is how he sees it, Mr. Horne. You are present at a moment of cinema history. He is about to create – look, his features are getting all tortured – he's getting all worked up – the muse is fluttering about him, looking for a place to perch. There she is – go it, gel! There! She's lighted on his shoulder.

JULIAN I've got it!

SANDY He's got it, Mr. Horne. It's coming over him in waves.

JULIAN We're going to do *Samson and Delilah.*

SANDY Go on, Jule, how do you see it?

JULIAN Well, I see Samson as huge and all butch, with great bulging thews and whopping great lallies, with long blond riah hanging right down his Jim and Jack –

SANDY That's rhyming slang for 'back'. Or, for France – 'down his Jules and Jim' – but I won't go into that. Yes – so what happens?

JULIAN I'll tell you what happens – the film opens with him lying there, spark out on his paliasse. Suddenly there's a movement behind the arras, and who comes trolling in but this palone Delilah. She vadas his sleeping eek, and she pulls out this pair of scissors and lops off his riah.

SANDY Yes. I can see that. Great close up of his head – nante riah. That's your cinema verite.

JULIAN Suddenly he comes round. 'Who's had me riah off?' he squeals. 'It's all ebbing away' – and then the Philistines come and mock him, Mr. Horne.

SANDY What a figure of tragedy he presents –

JULIAN Then they drag him up the king's lattie, and chain his lallies to a pillar. Then he gets his wild up, and with one mighty heave he brings the whole lattie tumbling about their heads. End of film.

SANDY Bravo, Jule, bravo! It's an Oscar winner. I shall go and go again. How about you, Mr. Horne?

HORNE Yes, it makes me want to go. And who do you see playing the role of Samson?

SANDY Well, let's see – the description says 'big, butch, muscular and blond'. There's only one person it can be.

HORNE Who's that?

SANDY It's *you,* Jules.

JULIAN That's a pity – I saw myself as Delilah.

BONA PRODS
PROD SAMSON AND DELILAH
SCENE 1
TAKE 97
SANDY

SANDY What with the decline in the cinema industry and the fact that we couldn't get financial backing, Jule never became a second Barbra Streisand, and then they repossessed our Bolex, so we got out of films and went in for travel. Reynard La Spoon, the choreographer, helped us to set up our own agency 'cos he was well in with Quantas – at least, that's what he said. We called it Bona Bijou Tourettes, and we'd hardly been in the place two minutes before Mr. Horne came trolling in.

Bona Bijou Tourettes

HORNE	I'm interested in booking a holiday.
JULIAN	Would you like us to do something exciting for you in a cheap package?
HORNE	Yes. What would you recommend?
SANDY	Well, how about Juan in the S of F? That's Les Pins. Bona, ennit Jule?
JULIAN	Divine. Sitting, sipping a tiny drinkette, vada-ing the great butch omis and dolly little palones trolling by, or disporting yourself on the sable plage getting your lallies all bronzed – your riah getting bleached by the soleil.
SANDY	That's your actual French. How about Juan Les Pins?
HORNE	I'm not besotted by Juan.
SANDY	He's not besotted, Jule. What else have we got in the S of F?
HORNE	Isn't it a bit expensive?
JULIAN	Oh, no. Not of you do it our way. We've got an ami down there who'll rent you his lattie.
SANDY	Who?
JULIAN	Gordon. You remember him.
SANDY	Oh, yes. That Gordon. Him with the leather jeans

and jackets and goggles and helmets and things. Looked like a kinky AA man. Him who had the bar in Tangiers?

JULIAN Yes. The Sheep's Eye in the Rue des Matelots.

SANDY Has he give up the bar?

JULIAN Yes. Fell through. She walked out on him.

SANDY What? The old American boiler?

JULIAN Yes. She *moved on.*

SANDY Hmm. Thought she would.

HORNE Sorry to interrupt you but if I hang about here much longer, my passport will expire.

SANDY Sorry. We was just having a wander down Memory Lane. Now – if we drop Gordon a little telegramette, I'm sure he'll accommodate you if we say you're a chum.

HORNE Somehow I don't think it's me. What else can you suggest?

SANDY Well, what else have we got with a little ambiance?

JULIAN Well, we've discovered a new place in Greece – right off the beaten. Village des naturistes – grass huts, volleyball in the starkers, folk singing and nut cutlets ... what more could you ask? Two weeks – fifty guineas.

HORNE All in?

JULIAN You probably would be after two weeks.

HORNE How about Spain? Somewhere like Malaga?

SANDY Don't talk to us about Malaga!

HORNE Naph, is it?

JULIAN He's got the palare off, hasn't he?

SANDY I should say it is naph, treashette. Jule had a nasty experience in Malaga.

JULIAN Traitor – you swore you'd never bring that up!

SANDY It was meaningful while it lasted but it's left its scars, hasn't it, Jule? And every time anyone mentions Malaga it wells up in him. You see, he got badly stung.

HORNE Portuguese man-of-war?

JULIAN Never found out what army he was in. Anyway, we wouldn't want you coming to grief in Malaga.

HORNE What else is there?

SANDY Well, all we got left on our books is Working Holidays – you can go coal-mining in the Ruhr, mackerel-gutting in Oslo, or sheep-shearing in Australia. Or there's one nearer home – Hamburg – that's very cheap.

HORNE I'll take it.

SANDY There is one slight drawback. Your day's your own, but twice nightly you have to put on a goat skin and wrestle with a camel in mud.

HORNE Hmm. I'll think about it. But tell me, what brought you into the travel business in the first place?

JULIAN Well, we've always enjoyed cruising, haven't we, Sand?

SANDY Always. It's a sort of wanderlust with us. We once did a round-the-world troll in a lifeboat.

JULIAN It was the call of the sea, Mr. Horne. When I get it, I can't resist it.

SANDY He can't resist it. When he gets the call he's got to go. Haven't you, Jule?

JULIAN Like a shot. I'm off like a shot.

SANDY You see, we was in Southampton and the urge came upon us. I said to Jule, 'Why not?' Didn't I, Jule?

JULIAN He did, Mr. Horne. So I said, 'Well, I'm game.'

SANDY Oh, he is, Mr. Horne. There's no one gamier.

JULIAN So we set sail next day – in this lifeboat.

HORNE With no preparations?

JULIAN Oh, I'd had me hair done. Anyway, to cut a long story short, after several days at sea, where did we find ourselves? Nowhere.

SANDY We hadn't seen a buoy for ages – so we had no idea where we were. Of course, we had our sea lallies by then but if I told you what we suffered, you'd never believe it.

JULIAN Fourteen days we were exposed to the elements without a single tin of face cream.

SANDY We nearly cracked, didn't we, Jule?

HORNE Nervous tension?

SANDY No, dry skin. Then this great storm blew up.

JULIAN Blew up, it did. Between him and me. I thought he'd nicked my eyebrow tweezers.

HORNE Did you keep a record of the trip?

SANDY Of course – show him your nautical log, Jule.

JULIAN Here, listen: 'Eighth day – still no land to be vada'd anywhere. Rations low – down to last tins of paté. Twelfth day – no food. Sand raving. Fourteenth day – I went overboard.'

SANDY Oh, it was terrible, Mr. Horne. A gale blowing and me hanging on to me jib for dear life – spray dashing in me eek – salt caking my eyelashes. Suddenly I become aware Jule is screaming.

HORNE Department of No Surprise.

SANDY I look – and there he is in the water. I shouted 'Ome overboard!'

HORNE What did you do?

SANDY There was only one thing to do in a predicament like that – I fainted.

JULIAN I summoned up me last resources, stiffened up me sinews –

SANDY They do go limp in the water.

HORNE But did you manage to drag yourself up on deck?

JULIAN No, we dressed casual – sweaters and jeans. Oh, I see what you mean! Yes, I got back on board, more dead than alive.

SANDY But I resuscitated him. Give him artificial resuscitation. The kiss of life.

JULIAN It's not like the real thing – more like the kiss of death. But listen to this from the log: 'Twenty-fifth day – Dear Diary, Sand's in one of his moods again – I think he's going to pieces.' He started to wander, didn't you, Sand?

SANDY Yes, I wandered. I don't like to talk about it, Mr. Horne – it was terrible. I was babbling, wasn't I, Jule?

JULIAN	He was babbling of green fields, he was. And Earls Court. And she was rolling and pitching.
SANDY	We was shipping it green over the bows, and our gunnels were awash, weren't they, Jule?
JULIAN	Yes.
SANDY	And I do hate washy gunnels.
JULIAN	Then, on the sixtieth day, we was picked up – by the Purser.
HORNE	Purser? I thought you were in a lifeboat.
SANDY	We was. But it was strapped to the deck of the Q.E.2.

PURSER

JULIAN It was a sad day for Sand and me when the travel agency folded. For a time we didn't know which way to turn. Then Sand had one of his flashes. 'What *can't* fold?' he said. 'I don't know,' I said. 'What can't?' 'Mangare,' he said. 'Let's open a little place that has ambiance where we can serve gourmet food at simply outrageous prices.' So we did. Needless to say, Mr. Horne was one of our first customers. He just blew in one night for a blow out. Sand was dragged up as the maître d'hôtel and greeted him as to the manner born.

La Casserole De Bona Gourmet

SANDY Welcome to our bijou restaurantette.

HORNE So you're restaurateurs now.

JULIAN Yes. We took it up after our success writing about mangare in the glossies.

SANDY We're Bona Viveur of the Sunday supp.

JULIAN He's your sort of in-Clement Freud, and I'm a sort of germ Carrier. We don't do it for the money, just to oblige our chums. We get a lot of telly people in.

SANDY Reynard La Spoon, the choreographer, he's always in – likes our omi cooking.

JULIAN Then there's Pandro Wildebeeste, the television producer – does all those tough, hard-hitting documentaries about life on the coal-face, and steel-smelting in Sierra Leone. Lives in that little pink cottage round the corner.

SANDY He's always dropping in for Jule's speciality.

JULIAN He likes what I do with herbs, you see.

SANDY Jule and his herbs. He can do anything with a few herbs. It's a gift.

JULIAN Shut up.

SANDY No, it is – don't run yourself down, Jule. He's always denigrating himself, Mr. Horne.

JULIAN Well, don't be strange, Mr. Horne. Sit yourself down. Now, what do you fancy?

HORNE Well, could I have a vada at your entrées?

SANDY Oh, he's bold!

JULIAN Here's the menu.

Bona Mangare
POMMES FRITES with everything

HORNE Hmm. I see you've got lally of lamb on –

JULIAN Yes, lamb's nice – or there's your jugged riah. That's palare for hare.

SANDY We got it from our special charcuterie.

HORNE Charcuterie – your butcher?

JULIAN You think so? Must be the way I've had me hair done.

SANDY (*confidentially*) Vidal likes him to show his ears. Well, if you've got them you might as well show them – 'course, they stick out a bit. He daren't go out in a high wind.

JULIAN They don't stick out.

SANDY Oh yes they do. You lacquer them back – I've seen you at it.

JULIAN Traitor! You swore you'd never tell.

SANDY Well, Mr. Horne, what's it to be?

HORNE What do you suggest?

SANDY Well, to start with – artichoke, with perhaps your mini glassette of Chablis.

JULIAN Then how about corn on your actual cob?

HORNE Yes. That's not a bad idea.

SANDY He'll want a Macon with that.

HORNE Why?

SANDY I've seen you. You're a messy eater.

JULIAN Then for your main course there's your chich kebab –

SANDY *Very* chich. With a bottle of your Chateauneuf du Pape. That's your Pope's Newcastle. There, a meal fit for a queen.

JULIAN Yes, I fancy it myself. Right, now you don't mind waiting, do you?

HORNE Why – where are you going?

SANDY Out for dinner.

HORNE But –

SANDY Oh, we're not eating here, ducky, the food's atrocious.

SANDY Of course, mingling with the smart set as we were, it was only a step from the restaurant in Islington to full indulgence in all the traditional sports of the English Gentleomi: shootin', fishin', poncin' and huntin'. Remember the Carnaby Hunt, Jule?

JULIAN Do I? It's etched on my memory's tablets, it is. *Etched.* Mr. Horne was there, wasn't he?

SANDY Was he not! He'd read our ad in the Sundays – 'Come trolling after the fox in specially selected groups'. And the next morning there he was, popping his head round the door.

Bona Hunt

HORNE Hello – is there anybody there?

JULIAN Yoicks, tally-ho, ducky!

SANDY We are your actual Carnaby Hunt. Jule's MFH – I'm the Whipper In.

HORNE And very nice you look, too. How many of you are there in the hunt?

JULIAN Just Sand and me so far.

SANDY And, of course, Reynard.

HORNE The fox?

SANDY No, ducky. Reynard La Spoon, the choreographer – he's a close personal, ent he, Jule?

JULIAN An intime – you'll get on well with him. He's your type – all butch.

SANDY But questing. You must have seen his work. He does fantastic things on the television.

JULIAN You know, they all come trolling on in form-hugging black and do evocative things with chairs and ladders and planks of wood. He once done something with a bentwood chair that made Robert Helpman's eyes stand out like organ stops.

SANDY It was his own fault for standing so close. 'Course, Reynard's classical trained.

JULIAN Oh, yes. He's got your full classical.

SANDY Started in John Cranko's *Nutcracker* and worked his way up.

JULIAN He supported Dame Margot's Sleeping Beauty when Nureyev backed out.

HORNE And he's the only other member of the hunt, is he?

SANDY So far – but we're hoping to attract your show business clientèle.

HORNE And where do you hunt from?

JULIAN Oh, here – in Carnaby Street.

HORNE There can't be many foxes in Carnaby Street.

JULIAN No. Not foxes. There's not what you could call a plethora of foxes round here, but you still have the thrill of the chase.

HORNE The chase? But what can you find to chase in Carnaby Street?

SANDY He's very jejune, isn't he, Jule?

JULIAN It's a quality I admire in him. Would that I still had it. (*Sighs*) Où sont les neiges d'antan, Mr. Horne –

SANDY That's your actual philosphical French. Still, don't brood, Jule, you'll get lines.

JULIAN Now, Mr. Horne – you ready for the off?

HORNE Yes.

JULIAN Just put this Pink Coat on – and these breeches –

SANDY And these bijou bootettes. . . . Right, now you're all dressed.

HORNE What happens now?

SANDY We just wait here till we vada the quarry. Look, there he goes – after him.

HORNE But what about the horse?

SANDY What horse? Jump on Jule's back.

SANDY Yoicks, tally-ho!

BONA PRINCE CHA
Unisex
LORD LOVUS
BOUTIQUE

JULIAN So off we galloped, but it wasn't a fox. It turned out to be Mick Jagger in a fun fur, but it was good sport, and mingling with the Carnaby Street set, our taste soon became known over a wide area and we was always being called in to advise on tarting up people's latties. Well, if you've got it you might as well harness it, *I* think, and as I've always had a flair for décor Sand said 'Let's' and I said 'Why not?', so we set ourselves up as interior decorators. Of course, Mr. Ram Singh and Gordon actually did the decorating, but the grand design was Sand's and mine, and we called the firm Fabe Homes and Bona Gardens. Mr. Horne was always mad keen to be inner than in, and it wasn't long before we had the call to visit his little pied à terre (that's your actual French) to give it a good going over. Mr. Horne showed us round – and frankly our stomachs went over.

Fabe Homes and Bona Gardens

SANDY	Hello Mr. Horne, ducky. It's us – Jule and Sand.
HORNE	Look, you'd better come in before the neighbours see you. Now, this is my living-room.
SANDY	Ugh! Nasty!
HORNE	What's wrong with it?
SANDY	Well, it's a bit vintage years of Hollywood, isn't it. I couldn't live in a place like this, could you, Jule?
JULIAN	Oooh no – I couldn't be doing with that flocked wallpaper – that'll have to go for a start. Gives me the horrors, it does. Oooh – ugh – I shall have to go and have a lie down.
SANDY	Now look what you've done to him. You might have had the place redecorated before you called us round here. See, when he sees wallpaper like that it completely clogs up his self-expression. Never mind, Jule, you can express yourself on his drapes.
JULIAN	Yes, we've got some bona curtain materials.
SANDY	Yes, fabe! Show him your swatch.
JULIAN	Yes – now, you have your plum velvet, you have your hessian, you have your silk –
HORNE	Wild?
SANDY	Absolutely insane!

JULIAN Then you have your various florals – your rhododendrons entwined with forget-me-nots, your creeping ivy, then you have your dandelion. Take your pick.

HORNE No, I wouldn't pick a dandelion; you know what they say. No – I fancy something a little different.

JULIAN Well, it's all down to black leather then.

HORNE Black leather curtains?

JULIAN Very kinky.

SANDY And if they wear, you can always have them half-soled and heeled.

SANDY Yes – put him down for leather curtains. 'Course, it means all that tat furniture'll have to go. It's quite out of keeping. What do you fancy, Jule?

JULIAN I see Danish teak everywhere.

SANDY Fabe!

JULIAN A touch of Victoriana – say a chaise longue or a what-not. Do you fancy a what-not in the corner, Sand?

SANDY Well, you want me to be frank, don't you? I mean, you like me to be blunt. You know me – tell the truth and shame the devil – well, frankly, man to man, I'm not besotted with the idea. It doesn't sing.

HORNE Well, that's a relief anyway. I don't think I could have stood a singing what-not.

JULIAN Wait a minute, wait a minute. It's coming to me, it's coming to me. I've got it, I've got it – Palais de Versailles – gilt caryatids, full-length mirrors, chandeliers.

SANDY Oh fantabulosa! Yes, but I think that ceiling'll have to go – it won't fit in.

JULIAN Yes, and that wall'll have to go – that don't fit in, neither.

SANDY Let's face it, Jule – everything'll have to go – I mean, none of it fits in. Right, that's settled then. Now let's have a vada at this garden of yours.

HORNE It's through here . . . .

SANDY	Ugh! Nasty! I couldn't be doing with a garden like this, could you, Jule? I mean, all them horrible little naph gnomes – ooh – ugh!
JULIAN	Oh no – it's a bit Noddy in Toyland, ennit? All that grass – that'll have to go – I mean, *grass* in a *garden,* Sand?
SANDY	Oh, très passé. The mind boggles.
HORNE	What do you suggest?
JULIAN	Paving, that's the answer here – paving.
HORNE	Crazy?
SANDY	Absolutely insane! Or you have your various types of stone.
JULIAN	Yes, you have your Florentine marble –
SANDY	Comes lovely in Florentine marble –
JULIAN	Or you have your ceramics.

SANDY Oh, fabe ceramics – all hand done by a disciple of William Morris in Ladbroke Grove. Or, Jule, wait a minute, how do you see his patio?

JULIAN Wait a minute, wait a minute, it's all happening in here. I've got it – terrazzo!

SANDY Oh, fantabulosa! Yes – and then maybe I could do something wild with a couple of creepers up his trellis. Yes, yes! I'm beginning to see it now. Go on, Jule.

JULIAN Er – let's see – what about something decadent? A sunken birdbath?

HORNE I'm afraid I don't know any sunken birds.

SANDY: Oh, bold! Yes, go on – it's beginning to sing to me now.

JULIAN Don't rush me, don't rush me – it's beginning to come over me in waves. I see it as a miniature version of the piazza in Florence.

SANDY Oh, it's a breakthrough! Mr. Horne, he's broken through. No – no – wait a minute – no – it won't work –

HORNE Why?

SANDY Well, you can't have a mock Tudor house with an Italianate piazza out the back.

HORNE Well, what do you suggest we do?

SANDY Only one thing for it. The house'll have to come down!

SANDY Mr. Horne got quite surly after that little incident and we didn't see him for some time. In fact, the next time we *did* see him was when we'd set up as tattooists. I won't go into the details of why we'd become tattooists except that Jule's friend, Jock, had come home from the sea covered in a riot of exotic designs – you should have *seen* his hanging gardens of Babylon – and we thought, well, the next trend's bound to be tattoos, so we got a quantity of Indian ink and some needles and set up shop. Next day, there was Mr. Horne on our doorstep. He was hardly inside the door before he blurted out his secret desires.

Bona Tattoos

HORNE	I hear that tattooing is the latest craze and I wanted something like Steve McQueen.
JULIAN	Well, everyone to his taste. How do you fancy a loyal slogan like 'England forever' or 'I love Malcolm Muggeridge'?
SANDY	We did that one the other day on this chap.
HORNE	Which chap?
SANDY	Malcolm Muggeridge.
HORNE	I thought I'd have something a little more intellectual.
JULIAN	Yes, Sand. He lends hisself to something more cultural. How do you fancy the Dead Sea Scrolls down his back?
SANDY	No – he don't want to cover hisself with a lot of posh chat in Hebrew – he wants something with a bit of life in it. I tell you what I'd like to see – he could have scenes from Disney – Jiminy Cricket crawling up his left leg, Donald Duck scampering down his right leg –
JULIAN	Yes, and Snow White and the Seven Dwarfs marching round his middle and disappearing down his trousers.

SANDY No, on second thoughts, it's a bit fey, isn't it? A bit whimsical. We can't decide really till we see what he could take. Get your shirt off and let's have a vada at you.

JULIAN Yes, come on – let the dog see the rabbit.

HORNE Just a moment then. Right. There. What do you think?

SANDY Well, you've got the area, I'll say that. Room to work. How do you think he'd take the Death of Nelson across his back?

JULIAN Oh, fabe! And we could incorporate that mole as Nelson's eyepatch. . . .

HORNE Well, I didn't think this would come up, but it's not actually a mole – it's a beauty spot.

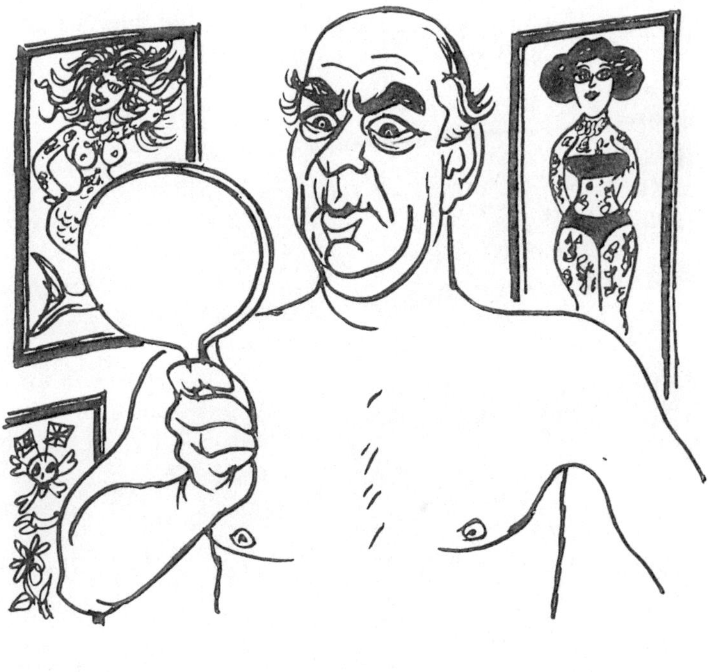

SANDY Oh, get him! The vanity of the man. Well, p'raps not Nelson, then. How about reproductions of great masterpieces?

JULIAN A bona idea. Now, let me see. . . .

SANDY He's pondering. He's trying to find it – he's got it – it's coming through – it's arrived – it's here – he's found it!

JULIAN I see a Botticelli. No, no, not a Botticelli – p'raps an El Greco. No, wait a minute – I see him with a tiny but perfect Watteau.

HORNE Yes – I've often been complimented on it.

SANDY Jule – I'm not besotted by it. I think he'd take the Mona Lisa well. We could have her peeping through the holes in his string vest, smiling enigmatically. Yes, that's what we'll do – the Mona Lisa.

HORNE What happens if I get tired of it?

SANDY You just pop back here. Jule will tattoo a moustache on her and, hey presto – you have your Laughing Cavalier.

CRUDE WORK REMOVED
DAME NELLIE DE RUNEHA

SANDY By the time he did come back, we'd moved on. We'd had a little trouble with the landlord. He wanted 'I love Bertha' with hearts entwined and a snake rampant up his arm, only unfortunately we run out of ink and it finished up reading 'I love Bert' and his missus hit him with the mangle. But we'd got a bit fed up anyway and the muse of terpsichore was calling and we decided to go back to our first love – the ballet.

JULIAN We were never at the Garden, you understand, but Sand and me had learned our trade with the Dame Nellie de Grunewald Company (Highly recommended at the Doncaster Festival de Terpsichore, 1954) and enfin, as they say, we started our own little troupe. Just Sand and me. We called it the Ballet Bona, and when Mr. Horne heard we'd been asked to appear in the Balls Pond Road Festival of the Arts, he naturally trolled round to see us at our rehearsal suite over the eel and pie shop in Shoe Lane.

Ballet Bona

HORNE	So you're the Ballet Bona now?
JULIAN	Yes. I'm Julinski and this is my friend, Sandeyev.
SANDY	Well, how nice to vada your eek again, Mr. Horne. What brings you trolling in here?
HORNE	I heard you were presenting a new ballet. Could you tell me something about it?
JULIAN	Yes – it's called *L'Après-midi d'un Goose.*
SANDY	That is your actual French, with the exception of goose, and we don't know the French for that. It means your goose's afternoon. That is the actual translation, isn't it, Jule?
JULIAN	Yes. That is your actual –
SANDY	Translation.
JULIAN	Yes. You see, we're bilingual. We've been suivezing la piste on the telly every Friday. Does wonders for your bon mots.

HORNE Why goose?

SANDY Why not?

HORNE Well, surely it should be *L'Après-midi d'un Faun.*

SANDY Well, you see, we went up the costumiers but they didn't have no fauns' costumes left. All they had was a goose left over from panto. It's actually got a trapdoor in it for dropping your golden egg out of, but we're not using that. It lacks poetry – among other things.

JULIAN 'Course, the big drawback is that it's a second-hand goose, you see. I mean, you don't know who's been in there. Still, you have to suffer for your art, don't you?

HORNE Well, what actually is the story of the ballet?

SANDY Well, you see, Jule here is the Goose King and I'm a hunter – Prince Roderick the Mighty. And I'm trolling through the forest one day and I come across this lovely creature –

JULIAN That's me.

SANDY He looks better in the skin. So anyway, I vada this goose cruising about on this magic pool. So what happens? I'll tell you what happens – all me hunting instincts rise, and I whip out me crossbow, do a pas de chat all around the stage, very butch-like, then I take aim and fire – and transfix him with me magic barb. Then he does the Dance of the Dying Goose.

HORNE I'd like to see him. Do you think he'd do it for me now?

SANDY Ask him, ducky.

HORNE Would you die for me?

JULIAN Gladly.

SANDY There he goes. He's dying now. Look at him flapping away. Flap, flap, flap, go on, gel! Oh, it's very pathetic, isn't it?

HORNE You took the word right out of my mouth.

JULIAN (*grunts and groans as he prances about*)

SANDY There he goes – he's going now – it's ebbing away.

No, wait a minute, it's coming back. No, he's going again, look, look – the way he's all curled up in a little ball – ah, bless him.

JULIAN (*bellows with pain*)

SANDY What's up?

JULIAN I've got me beak caught up me trapdoor. Hang on a minute. Right. Now, with a final flutter of my broken wings, I stagger back to the magic pool and plunge in.

SANDY Filled with remorse, I leap into the pool after him and after a breathtaking pas de deux, we expire together. The whole dénouement smacks more than a little of the definitely fantabulosa.

JULIAN 'Course, we know that we're a little far out. We're only on the fringe, as it were.

HORNE Of the festival?

JULIAN Oh, yes. *And* of the festival. But if we get the critical acclaim we deserve, it'll mean a world tour – Monte Carlo, the Lincoln Centre, the Bolshoi, Covent Garden –

HORNE And if it doesn't succeed?

SANDY Well, I s'pose it's back to washing up at the Corner House.

JULIAN I had to give up the ballet. That goose skin gave me claustrophobia – among other things – and for a time, Sand and me was hard put to it to know what to do next. Then we thought, 'Why not all-in wrestling?' I missed the music at first, but otherwise the transition was easy, as ballet and wrestling are not dissimilar. At least, not in the way Sand and me approached the noble art of the grapple. So anyway, we were practising our cross-buttocks in Wally Goatsbreath's gym one day when Mr. Horne popped in.

Bona Grapplers

HORNE	Hello – anybody there?
JULIAN	Oh hullo, I'm Julian and this is my friend, Sandy.
SANDY	Or, to use our ring names, Man Mountain Jule and Sky High Sand. But what brings you trolling in here?
HORNE	Well, I believe you're experts on wrestling – I wondered if you could fill me in?
JULIAN	Oh, yes. Apart from wrestling ourselves, we are entrepreneurs.
SANDY	That is your actual French. Jule and me have handled all the top grapplers at one time or another. Take the Hooded Terror – he's one of ours. The Iron Man, he's one, too. Then there's the Borneo Maniac – comes on as a gorilla.
JULIAN	Oh, her! She's too much, she is.
HORNE	*Her?*

SANDY I thought everybody knew. Alice Makepeace, her name is. Used to wrestle in mud and we made the mistake of signing her up before we'd scraped her off.

JULIAN Was our eeks red when it turned out to be a palone!

HORNE That accounts for her wearing a gorilla skin.

SANDY Oh, it's not a skin. It's natural, that is.

HORNE But you do actually wrestle yourselves?

JULIAN Not actually ourselves. Each other. You may have seen us last Saturday afternoon on telly.

HORNE Yes, I did.

SANDY Well, what did you think of our performance? You can be frank. Be as brutal as you like – we can take it. You think it lacked, don't you? You wasn't besotted.

HORNE Well –

JULIAN We didn't come across, did we?

HORNE No.

SANDY You see, Jule, what did I tell you? It's that television director. Got no idea. Couldn't shoot a cross-buttock to save his life.

JULIAN And his camera angles – all to pot! Kept dollying in on me bad side. You see, from the wrong angle I look almost plain –

SANDY No, you don't.

JULIAN I do. I know it. My knees in a close-up look dead naph. I mean, let's face it, they're wrinkled. I've tried everything – creams, astringent lotions; I've had 'em lifted twice, but there's no doing anything with them knees of mine. I think wrinkled knees are so ugly in a wrestler, don't you?

HORNE But surely appearances aren't all that important.

SANDY You must be joking, ducky – that's what the women come to see. They come to have a vada at two great huge brawny men battling it out. That's why I cover meself all over in oil – it enhances me physique.

JULIAN I wish you wouldn't do it, though. You keep slipping out of me hammer-lock.

HORNE	Well, they say that a lot of wrestling is phoney – is that true?
SANDY	Oh, no. Last week, for instance, me and Jule had a real *grudge* fight. We both got our wilds up in the third.
JULIAN	Well, you started it, hogging the close-ups like that.
SANDY	Maybe, ducky, but that's no excuse for what you did. It was brutal, Mr. Horne – bestial – what he done.
HORNE	What happened?
SANDY	He grabbed me by the wrist, pinned me down, and then broke it.
HORNE	Your wrist?
SANDY	No, ducky, me fingernail!

SANDY Jule and me have always been interested in the law. Well, Jule takes silk very well and I've always fancied myself in a wig. Not only that, but we've had a lot of experience in court – one way or another – and one day we thought, 'Why not have a practice in Lincoln's Inn?', so we did, and after *that* little misunderstanding was cleared up, we opened a bijou law firm – and would you believe it, Mr. Horne was our first client. I'll never forget his woebegone eek as he sat in our chambers and unburdened himself. . . .'

Bona Law

HORNE Can you help me? I've erred.

SANDY Well, we've all erred, ducky. I mean, it's common knowledge, ennit, Jule?

HORNE Will you take my case?

JULIAN Well, it depends on what it is. We've got a criminal practice that takes up most of our time.

HORNE Yes, but apart from that – I need legal advice.

SANDY Ooh – isn't he bold? Time has not withered nor custom staled *his* infinite variety.

JULIAN What is it you've done?

HORNE (*shyly*) I don't like to say.

JULIAN Oh, you can tell us. Sand and me have handled the most bizarre briefs – nothing could shock us.

HORNE Well – look, it's here on this charge sheet.

SANDY Let's have a vada. Oh Jule, look at this!

JULIAN Ooh! He didn't!

SANDY He did. Look, it's written down.

JULIAN But I mean – in broad daylight – outside the Corner House – aren't you ashamed?

BONA LAW
COMMISSIONERS FOR MILD OATHS
CHUMS
PICK OF PUNCH
BOYS OWN PAPER
TORTS
RETORTS

HORNE Yes – but it is only a parking offence.

SANDY *Only!* They're very hot on that. What do you think, Jule?

JULIAN Hmm – let me look up me tort.

SANDY Shh – he's looking up his tort. Sometimes it takes him hours to find what he's looking for. Ah, he's found it. Well?

JULIAN I recommend we try *Per verulium ad camphorum actus injuria linctus est.*

SANDY That's your actual Latin.

HORNE What does it mean?

JULIAN I dunno – I got it off a bottle of horse rub, but it sounds good, doesn't it? How shall we tackle it, Sand?

SANDY I think we should plead insanity.

JULIAN Yes, but what about Mr. Horne?

SANDY Oh, him. I'll defend him. I'll do me speech for the defence. Would you like to hear it?

JULIAN Go on, do your plea, Sand. Oh, he's an eloquent pleader.

SANDY Omes and palones of the jury, vada well the eek of the poor ome who stands before you, his lallies trembling. He has his share of guilt, but who is without it? We all have a bit – every one of us. We have our share. His only crime was that he loved not wisely but not too well. This kid never had a chance – born on the wrong side of the tracks, forced to take in washing – society drove him to a life of vice. It is not this ome who is on trial – it is all of us. We made him what he is – without hope, without love, without hair. Give him a chance to become a useful citizen again – a housewife and a mother, so that he can look the world in the face and say, 'I name this ship HMS Ark Royal. God bless all who sail in her!'

JULIAN Bravo, Sand! You could have been a Queen's Counsel. Well, Mr. Horne – what do you say?

HORNE Have you got Quintin Hogg's phone number?

SANDY When did we meet Mr. Horne next, Jule?

JULIAN I think it was after you were disbarred and before we went into our next big venture. We was filling in at that pet shop.

SANDY So we were, and Mr. Horne come in looking for a pet and we was all covered in hair.

JULIAN Oh yes, I remember. We'd been stripping a borzoi.

SANDY Well, we *thought* it was a borzoi but when we'd stripped him it turned out he was just a hairy whippet.

JULIAN Anyway, right in the middle of all that, in came Mr. Horne.

HELLO
SAILOR

Bona Pets

SANDY Hello, Mr. Horne – what brings you trolling in?

HORNE Well, actually I'm looking for a pet.

SANDY Well, of course, dogs are nice, don't you think, Jule?

JULIAN Oh yes, we've got a plethora of dogs here. How do you fancy a little chihuahua?

HORNE No thanks. I don't smoke.

SANDY Oh, bold! No, he means a Mexican Hairless. I should have thought that was very suitable for *you.* Or you have your poodle. That's a noble beast, isn't it, Jule?

JULIAN Yes. And you can have 'em in any colour you like. You have your blue rinse, your grey rinse – you can have any colour to match your barnet.

SANDY Now we're back on the Mexican Hairless again.

JULIAN No, I tell you what, we got one poodle – very unusual shade, he's streaked with lavender and crimson. We didn't intend it that way, but he rolled

Julian

in the paint while we was doing the bathroom. He's a very eye-catching little fellow, though.

SANDY No, he's not the poodle type, Jule. A poodle's not really *him*.

HORNE Well, what sort of dog would you recommend?

JULIAN Well, we've got some new strains we've bred ourselves. There's Cyril – he's half-and-half, you know. Half King Charles spaniel, half fox terrier. We call him a fox-cocker.

SANDY Or you can have your Doberman wolfhound, your wire-haired dalmatian – or then, there's Queenie. She's a cross between a German sausage dog and a greyhound.

HORNE A sort of grey sausage doghound?

JULIAN Yes. She stands four foot high with her belly dragging on the ground. She may not look much but she don't half go.

HORNE It's not exactly what I had in mind – I was looking for something a little more exotic.

SANDY Would you like a Peke?

HORNE I don't really think so – but what about this little chap on the counter? He seems very quiet and well behaved. Yorkshire terrier, isn't he?

SANDY Not exactly. It's a floor mop.

HORNE Yes, I thought he had rather a long tail.

SANDY Are you absolutely set on a dog?

HORNE No, not really. I just wanted something out of the ordinary.

JULIAN Well, how about our twin set? Hamster and tortoise? Marvellous for dealing with burglars.

HORNE What? A hamster and a tortoise? How?

JULIAN Well – the burglar creeps in through the window – sees the hamster sitting there wrinkling his nose and looking all cute – so he gives a squeal of delight, and while he's bending down going 'Kootchy kootchy koo', you creep up behind him and hit him with the tortoise.

JULIAN The pet shop was only a fill-in really. We were never ideally suited to it. What with me being allergic to budgies and Sandy not being able to bear mice, we spent our time there with me sneezing and coming out in unsightly blotches, and Sand standing on a chair, screaming.

When we got the chance to run a language studio we leapt at it. We thought it would be a gold-mine, what with the Common Market and everyone going abroad and all the illegal immigrants and everything. Well, we started with high hopes in a room in Earl's Court and it wasn't long before Mr. Horne turned up. And I don't tell no lies when I say it was bona to vada his dolly old eek again that day he came trolling in.

Bona Palare

HORNE	So you're French teachers now?
JULIAN	Oh, oui – we are your actual maîtres des langues.
SANDY	He don't tell no lies. Our motto – 'You're never alone on a foreign strand, with a language taught by Jule and Sand.'
JULIAN	How can we help you, visage de coeur?
SANDY	That's French for 'heartface'.
HORNE	Oh – well, for a start I'd like to brush up my Greek.
SANDY	Don't let us stop you if it gives you pleasure.
HORNE	The Greek *language*.
JULIAN	Oh – well, we're not too hot on Greek. To be honest, we don't know our alpha from our omega. All he knows is shish kebab and all I know is the Acropolis.
SANDY	By moonlight – he had an experience up the Acropolis, didn't you, Jule?

JULIAN	I'd rather not speak of it.
SANDY	I'm not surprised. He could tell you things, Mr. Horne, that'd make Lawrence Durrell sound like Patience Strong.
HORNE	Are you by any chance referring to Lawrence Durrell's *Tunc*?
SANDY	No – I never repeat gossip.
HORNE	Now, where were we?
SANDY	Up the Acropolis.
JULIAN	Frankly, we're not dab hands at your Greek.
HORNE	What *do* you specialize in?
JULIAN	Well, we concentrate on modern languages – French, Italian, Spanish – for the holiday-maker.
SANDY	Though we do the more exotic tongues if you wish them.
HORNE	Such as?
JULIAN	Cambodian, Tibetan, Australian. . . .
SANDY	And we can give you a smattering of Afghan. Not much – but enough to get you through the Khyber.
JULIAN	Then we do your various Chinese dialects – Cantonese, Cochinese, Pekinese –
HORNE	Pekinese? How does that sound?
JULIAN	Would you believe, 'Woof woof'?
SANDY	And then, of course, we specialize in English for the foreign visitor.
JULIAN	We're working on an old Sikh now.
SANDY	Ram Singh. He didn't speak a word when he come to us – but you should hear him now. Fetch him out of the cubicle, Jule – introduce him to Mr. Horne.
JULIAN	(*calls*) Mr. Ram Singh – we'd like you to meet a friend.
SANDY	This is Mr. Horne.
HORNE	How do you do.
SINGH	Hello, Mr. Horne, ducky – how bona to vada your dolly old eek.
SANDY	He's got all the palare, ent'he?
HORNE	Yes – he's a sort of Jule of the Orient.

SANDY Oh, bold! Alright, Mr. Ram Singh, back to the cubicle, ducky.

HORNE Cubicle?

JULIAN Yes, it's our method – soundproof cubicle and headphones.

SANDY Then we play you gramophone records of the language of your choice.

JULIAN We've patented the method – we call it Palarephone.

SANDY Yes, it's our method. Jule has devoted his life to perfecting the method, haven't you, Jule?

JULIAN I have.

SANDY Tell him how you started.

JULIAN On the method?

SANDY Yes.

JULIAN I don't like to.

SANDY That's your trouble, Jule – you won't push yourself. He's shy, you see – it's his shyness that's held him back. I keep telling him he's got to push himself. It's being the only child, you see – it's made him withdrawn.

JULIAN I'm nervous with strangers.

HORNE Well, I'm not strange.

SANDY Oh – get him! Go on, Jule, tell him how it all started.

JULIAN Well – I had this friend –

SANDY Friend – yes –

JULIAN In the merchant navy, and every time he come into port he'd bring me something. A ukelele or a ship in a bottle.

SANDY He was generosity itself, he was – Jock. He used to make the ships in bottles himself, didn't he, Jule? You'd be amazed what Jock could do with a bit of wood and a bottle.

JULIAN Yes – that's one of his on the mantelpiece.

HORNE Well, I can see the bottle, but there's nothing in it.

JULIAN No, it's the Marie Celeste. So, any road up, one leave he brought me a parrot.

SANDY And this parrot could speak seventeen languages.

STRIP TEASE
LE BISTRO
ESPRESSO
BOOKS MAGS
SUZETTE
FRENCH LESSONS
1st Floor
BONA LINGO
YOUR ACTUAL

HORNE A polyglot.

JULIAN Yes – so I thought if a dumb beast could do it, so could I.

SANDY And that's how it started – and today Jule can say 'Polly wants a cracker' in every language in the world.

JULIAN So we started this school.

HORNE What a fascinating story – he said, lying in his teeth.

SANDY So what language would you like to learn, Mr. Horne?

HORNE Well, I think perhaps Spanish.

SANDY Hmm, yes, alright then – we'll start you off with lesson one. Here's a list of Spanish phrases and what they mean in English. You learn these for a start.

JULIAN They're useful phrases for the traveller.

HORNE What's this? 'Good morning, good afternoon, good night. Hello. I cannot speak Spanish. Please write it down. I am lost. This man is pestering me. Fetch a policeman. I have lost my handbag.' *I've lost my handbag?* I thought you said these were useful phrases for the traveller. What use is that?

SANDY Well, *we* found it useful when *we* was in Spain!

SANDY — Nice as the Ecole des Langues was, we missed show business, didn't we, Jule?

JULIAN — Missed it, yes.

SANDY — So we converted, didn't we?

JULIAN — We did. You don't tell no lies.

SANDY — We started a little theatrical agency. We did cabarets mostly – discreet entertainments for those in quest of select titillation of a refined nature.

JULIAN — Yes. We sent out a brochure which said, 'Whatever your function, Julian and Sandy can sprinkle it with stardust.'

SANDY — And, of course, we soon had a tickle from Mr. Horne.

JULIAN — I can remember to this day how he come into the office looking all butch and masterful.

Bona Performers

HORNE Look, you two – I've been asked to organize a cabaret for the BBC on the fifteenth. I was wondering if you could fix me up.

SANDY Oh yes, ducky. We'd be glad to fix you up anytime. BBC, is it? Oh, you'll want something a bit risqué for that mob. How about Queenie? I think she's at liberty.

HORNE What does Queenie do?

JULIAN Striptease with a difference. See, normally she's the Bearded Lady at Blackpool. Long beard, she's got, right down to her ankles.

SANDY And instead of stripping, she just come on and shaves. She can't do it often. It takes her two years to grow the beard again, poor love.

HORNE It's not exactly what I had in mind. A little less exotic, I think.

JULIAN Well, would you like to have a leaf through me files? See if there's anyone you fancy?

SANDY Yes – Jule, get out your immediate vacancies and let the gentleman have a vada.

JULIAN How about him? Nemesis Groatblast – England's Premier Yodelling Archbishop. He's VAF, you know.

HORNE Variety Artistes' Federation?

SANDY Oh, is that what it means? We thought it meant 'Vada! Absolutely Fantabulosa!'

HORNE And what does he do?

JULIAN Well, it's difficult to describe, but it involves feats of incredible agility and dexterity with a fire extinguisher, a frankfurter sausage and a goat.

SANDY Yes. Unfortunately, though, the goat's got a prior engagement on the fifteenth. But we can get you the Great Omipaloni – he's one of ours, isn't he, Jule?

JULIAN Oh, yes. He's your actual strong man. Beggars description, he does.

HORNE Could you give me some idea of his act?

SANDY Well, he comes on wearing this leopard skin, see – he's a great huge butch ome, with thews like an oak and bulging lallies –

JULIAN Then he bends an iron bar – tears two telephone directories in half, drives a nail through a plank with his bare fist, and then, as a finale, for his pièce de résistance –

SANDY That's your actual French –

JULIAN He's harnessed between two teams of wild horses – pulling in opposite directions. But does he budge? Budge he does not! We bill him as the strongest man on earth.

HORNE I'll take him, then.

SANDY But you can't have him on the fifteenth. That's his night for washing his hair.

HORNE Well, who else have you got that's available?

JULIAN Well, *we're* available, aren't we, Sand?

SANDY Extremely. We'll be happy to oblige on the fifteenth. We are your great all-round entertainers – Sand and Jule – a show in theirselves – the brightest stars in the show business firmament. We can be seen nightly at the Marine Commando Club in Paddington, can't we, Jule?

JULIAN Yes. Come and see us. Drag yourself up there one night. We have to be seen to be believed.

HORNE And what, I shudder to ask, do you do?

SANDY Oh, bold! He goes too far, doesn't he? Well, we are versatile, Mr. Horne. You name it – we do it.

HORNE Do you tell jokes?

JULIAN No. We have no flair for comic banter.

HORNE Tap dance?

SANDY No. We don't do your actual wallop.

HORNE Juggle?

JULIAN No.

HORNE Conjure?

SANDY No.

HORNE I thought you said if I named it you could do it?

SANDY Ah, yes, ducky – but you haven't named it yet.

HORNE Well, one last desperate throw of the dice – do you sing?

JULIAN *Sing?* In our circle we're known as the second Peters and Lee.

SANDY Yes. He sings like Mary Peters and I sound like Lee Remick.

JULIAN Hmm – nice.

HORNE Well, I've got to provide some entertainment. Will you do it?

SANDY Of course we will. Would you like a quick vada at our repertoire? Jule, position yourself at the upright. We'll give Mr. Horne our selection of camp-fire songs. Right, after two.

JULIAN (*sing*) I dream of Jeannie with the light brown riah –
SANDY

JULIAN (*sings*) Bless this lattie strong and stout,
Keeping all naph omes out –

JULIAN
SANDY (*sings*) I'll troll beside you through the world today

BALLS POND ROAD
Empire
JULIAN & SANDY
Horner

JULIAN (*sings*) Someday she'll troll along,
The palone I love –
Maybe I shall meet her Monday –
Maybe Tuesday –

SANDY No, not Tuesday. You've got the hairdressers –

JULIAN Oh yes.

SANDY He goes to the same one as Kojak. . . .

JULIAN
SANDY (*sing*) Oh, he flies through the air with the greatest of ease –
The daring young ome on his flying trapeze,
His eek is so bona
All palones he does please –
And my love he has stolen away.

SANDY After that, we do our pièce de résistance that smacks not a little of the definitely fantabulosa –

JULIAN (*sings*) There's a hole in my bucket,
Dear Sandy, dear Sandy,
There's a hole in my bucket,
Dear Sandy, a hole.

SANDY (*sings*) Then why don't you block it,
Dear Julian, dear Julian,
Then why don't you block it,
Dear Julian, block it?

JULIAN (*sings*) With what shall I block it,
Dear Sandy, dear Sandy,
With what shall I block it,
Dear Sandy, with what?

SANDY (*sings*) If I were to tell you,
Dear Julian, dear Julian,
If I were to tell you –
We'd wind up in court.